THE IVY HIDES
THE FIG-RIPE DUCHESS

for Richard and Lewis, with love

THE IVY HIDES
THE FIG-RIPE DUCHESS

ELLIE EVANS

SEREN

Seren is the book imprint of
Poetry Wales Press Ltd.
57 Nolton Street, Bridgend, Wales, CF31 3AE
www.serenbooks.com

ISBN: 978-1-85411-546-1

A CIP record for this title is available from the British Library.

The publisher acknowledges the financial assistance of the Welsh Books Council.

Cover art: Green Metaphor by Ceri Richards
Image © Artists's Estate and Martin Tinney Gallery

Printed in Bembo by The Berforts Group Ltd, Stevenage

Contents

Skin

I am not easy in my skin
which fits too tight
like a drum stretched thin
where others beat
and sing.

They say that I must grow
a thicker skin
but I know
that you'll get under,
worm within, and so

I'll cast it off and jump outside,
use it as vellum
to write and hide.
All flesh is dust, they say,
all dust is skin.

Seeing Straight

Although the railway
cuts the skyline
with a T-square's
neatness, left
to itself, nature
would be curved:
everything is bent
by wind or rain
or gravity,
the surge of sap
or the beat of blood.
Sky and sea
meet in an arc:
the only straight
lines are inside
your head, when
you join your dots up.
Dots, please note,
have no space
at all, and the lines
you make no thickness.
They won't make a net
to support your weight,
you can't swing
from them. But they
are your railroad slicing
through barley, your arrow
to the sunset. Then,
zig-zag between
the stars: devise
your templates.

The Ivy Hides the Fig-ripe Duchess

sheathed in a tuxedo of meteorites

After the first purges, the fields were full of corpses
whose nails went on growing, curling into the earth like sickles.
Crows sat on these cadavers and feasted,
beginning with their eyes.

After the second, all the books were dumped –
their leaves fluttered off into the forest
while a heap of computers winked at the vultures
who blunted their beaks on the screens.

And then some monkeys found the typewriters,
still with blank paper in them. They'd seen it all before
and so they sat and typed. And typed. And typed.

It had all grown very quiet, the trees had shrivelled,
the rivers had run dry. Vulture and hyena
had long since eaten each other

and still the monkeys typed, their return bells
ringing across the valley, their pile
of writing rising and fading in the heat.

That's what was left: *'Tis bitter cold,*
and I am sick at heart.

Ant in Vaseline

Film noir favours underground scenes
like this still from *The Third Man* where arches
frame a sewer and light splinters on black water,
while men in trench-coats grasp their guns and wait.

My memories are subterranean too, grey light
and a white enamel table with black edges,
so sharp you could cut yourself.
That's where my father stoops over his machine,

a brass harpy. It has my mother's face,
her cold hard breasts; her wings and claws
are sticky. Her name is Celeno,
darkness. My father's fingers stroke her hair

as he bends her neck, tips the mirror
at her feet, with a twang slips
a wafer-sandwich made of glass
between the clips held in her lap.

He pulls my face down to the eyepiece,
the halo round her head. I watch. Those twitching
segments are my body, my legs no bigger
than an eyelash, scrabbling and slithering.

That's how I hurl myself, my jaws agape,
against my see-through ceiling,
see-through jelly walls,
my see-through floor.

Lilac

At eleven in the morning when the snow turns pink
a man in an astrakhan hat walks to a building
whose windows are black,

whose doors glide open on iron rails.
Down a slope he shuffles; in the dark
the concrete grates his fingers.

There are rooms stacked high with brown files,
a pile of suitcases and metal doors
with grilles that slide.

Some are missing, like teeth knocked out.
There are blisters on the wall
and scratches. The passage winds

to a table of permits
in one language, then another,
never his own. In a telephone box

the receiver hangs like a broken arm.
There are typewriters, wireless sets,
a small dinghy and photographs of girls in smocks

throwing roses. Was he the boy
behind the lilac, watching
the Cossacks dance?

Crazy House at the Fairground

Here's a room of snug banality:
a carpet swims with red chrysanthemums
and an apricot lampshade puffs like a tutu.
Beside the castellated fireplace
mother and father wait
in their belted mackintoshes.
She rests her head against his shoulder, nuzzles
the beige epaulette – his little dwarf.
See how they stamp their booted feet
when the music bumps and grinds and the walls shake,
see how they dance and then, like sentries, change place
so she's the tall one now, he's just the midget,
his head against her waist. How can this be,
when walls and ceilings seem so straight?

IKEA Room Set

No outside wall – you're straight onto a mat
(just like the one at home). The table's laid for four
with dark red plates and napkins, and there's more
scarlet in the stripy curtains. You see that
there's a saucepan on the stove, as though perhaps
someone was cooking, and stopped. Look, on the floor
a toy-train's wooden track leads to the door
where there's a wicker basket for the cat.

Yes, everything you see here on display
can be obtained down in the Service Hall
flat-packed. Of course we know our doors are false,
our windows blind. You take it all away,
you make it up at home and try to catch
our story. What you've got is mugs that match.

Edna

She was my father's unmarried sister
whom my mother mocked at Christmas, and hiccuped at,
demanding Edna went to the Spar for whisky and be quick about it.

Edna spent her weekday evenings at rainy bus-stops
after washing down the Cookery Room when her classes had gone.
Years later, girls would stop in the street and thank her

and she was proud she'd taught them Easter biscuits, invisible mending
and how to balance a budget. By then, her time was free
so she walked in Lapland to the Northern Lights,

found slipper orchids by the reservoir,
learnt at U3A about pie-crust tables.
She helped with the library trolley in the hospital ward

where, last Christmas, she was taken in for tests.
From the way she'd cough when she answered the phone,
lived on custard from Tesco, and Gaviscon, I should have guessed.

I'll tell you for why, my dear, she'd say,
when she asked me to change a bulb, or write to the bank.
Edna, it's my turn to tell you 'for why'. Thanks.

A Post-it on the Microwave

Everything around you crumbles: your papery hands,
the flakes of skin on your frayed collar,

the tea-leaves clogged in the sink's bend and,
as you turn to climb the stairs, you're smaller

than I'd thought, your shanks and buttocks shrunk
look, somehow, like an elephant's. You grope

and fumble under the Singer's twisted shank,
peering at the eyelet hole to thread the loop –

but your sewing days are over. Your stitches bobble,
the cotton is too taut. You turn the wheel

and it spins emptily. It's too much trouble,
so pack it all away. Even your meals

you don't cook, they come dished up in silver foil
and have no flavour, only taste of dust.

At least they're safe, no need to grill or boil.
On the microwave, a post-it aide memoire: *I must...*

Woodland Happy Families

Nobody sees butchers or carpenters now
or if you do, they're at computers
and wearing jeans. I suppose we could
have Chloe the Party Organiser,
Niobe the Loss Adjuster, but then
their nuclear groupings are too intertwined
to illustrate. No, escape
to the forest, where beds
have pink and yellow patchwork quilts
and stereotypes mean business.

Mr. Fox is a sporting toff,
cravat and monocle say it all;
his wife conceals a pheasant
in her basket, their son dangles
a catapult and little sister
raids the moneybox. Robins,
naturally, are in the snow
wearing tartan tam o'shanters;
I think the Owl is a Bank Manager,
the sort to have a Daimler.

All fathers are providers, laying up
acorns, digging tunnels. Mothers are stay-at-homes,
they sweep and shop, make pies from mice
or dote on tadpoles in their cribs.
Miss Badger's at her dressing-table
beneath the earth in candle-light;
(all little girls are nice, but vain). Wistfully
Miss Frog scans her How To book on wooing
while Miss Hedgehog admires a cactus.
Outside their brothers are at their pranks
but Master Owl's a dunce!

Not all the sets are whole:
we've lost two shrews, a squirrel
and a rabbit. It's hard to play properly
when you have to swap and shuffle.

They were Too Poor for Buttons

They were too poor for buttons, so her mother would collect
cherry stones, apricot kernels or conkers, and would crochet round them.
When she went cleaning she was given cast-off jumpers
which she unravelled and made up again, re-mixed, so Jean
had a cardigan blue as Quink ink, with yellow walnut buttons
and a scarlet rose in a mohair mix, that covered up a hole.

I sat beside Jean in Sunday School, admiring the silver paper
she'd saved from a cigarette packet and used to line her pencil box.
How I liked the lettuce-green of the blanket stitch around her cuffs,
but most of all, I envied her for the magic warts proud on her knuckles.

New Curate at Llanina

my grandfather: Eynon Hughes

Perhaps it was her voice he heard
at evensong, above the surf, the shriek
of gulls, sheep on the headland calling,
while her thin soprano trembled at the psalm;

or was it a tea-party, when he saw
the ink-blue veins twitching in her wrists
as she swept crumbs into a silver pan?
Meanwhile conversation stuttered, like the flies

trapped in the drawn-thread window nets, sewn
by her sister that very spring, just before she died.
At any rate, there must have been a courtship,
a stealthy prowl along those dripping lanes.

Acknowledged suitor, now he comes at twilight,
picking his way between the corn stooks
because he's carrying a tray of rings
which wink and sparkle as the darkness grows.

Sounds of Innocence and Experience

my grandmother: Edith Hughes

Standing on the doorstep, she heard fairy bells
ringing across the valley.
She didn't know about ice-cream vans.
Inside the dark house, Sunday smelt of sprouts and polish;
the radio thundered Welsh from cold grey chapels:
Tabernacle, Peniel, Moriah.

In the afternoon, she watched
from the doorway of the woodshed
while the hens screamed.
Her grandmother grasped a scaly neck,
aimed her long knife at a red frantic tongue,
rammed it, twisting, down the open throat.

In the warm cowshed, the milk frothed gently,
rippling down the wash-board separator.

Tinnitus Calling

A hidden wireless in a haybarn, that confident
and bowler-hatted voice: *London calling*,
summoning allies as the world dies, stashing
cargo-drops in football scores. Fingers swivel
the dial, hoping for sound-fall: Prague,
Jakarta, Budapest. Nothing, nothing
but a high-pitched radio whine, like the one
in my ear now. Tinnitus calling.

A micro-split of silence, slap of waves –
and then a cry of gulls, their yearning scream
that takes me back to childhood; submarines
all belly-up on a concrete beach,
a morning forecast in Hong Kong: *Pressure
is high in China and adjacent seas.*

Seedcorn

In Nutwood, Rupert's father wore a bracken-
coloured jacket when he did the garden;
his mother stayed indoors, in an apron

frilled like the mantelpiece. Bluebell woods
had winding paths which led him home again
after his visit to the elves, deep in their caves

where lanterns flamed with trapped sunshine.
On the next page you could make an elf
by folding paper on the dotted line.

One day in Bournemouth, my teenage heroine
hopped on a bus because she liked its name,
then spent a golden summer out of time;

the hidden house she camped in, she revived:
pulled paper off the wainscot, scrubbed it white,
trundled the mildewed chairs off-stage, repaired

a lacquered bed inlaid with tourmaline;
then, dead on cue, right on the final page
our hero returned to claim his lost domaine.

Jan Morris made up Hav from everywhere
she'd been: the iron dog from Venice, a bridge
from Newport in South Wales; she wove it all

together. We're the same, framed by the dots
we've joined as bandage, hammock, parachute.
We glut on stories, we slip between their lines

to sleep, still in their dream-mesh caught.
In a cocooned trance we are re-formed:
this is where we come from, how we make our home.

Two Monologues from *The Odyssey*

1. Kalypso

The distant line of mountains out to sea
are what you sit to look at every day:
they're like the gauzy veils of memory

your inward gaze is fixed on, not on me.
You're on the headland, weeping. Gray
the distant line of mountains out to sea

where Penelope, your wife, weaves faithfully.
That's the picture that you cling to, but I say
you too are weaving veils of memory.

Stay here with me! I've meadows of parsley
where we could lie, drink wine, not see the bay
or distant line of mountains out to sea.

Crunch time: our final night. I promise not to be
bitter, or cry. I want you to portray
me well, when you narrate this memory.

I load your raft with treasure, set you free.
You sail away. All stained with tears and spray
and now, just one more scrap of memory,
I gaze at your sharp mountains out at sea.

2. Odysseus

The braided goddess lets me go at last:
she loads my boat with wine, gold cloth and treasure –
and weeps. Although she'd like to hold me fast,
the braided goddess lets me go at last.
Just like those other girls met in the past
who punctuate this long and fraught adventure,
the braided goddess lets me go at last –
and loads my boat with *yet more* bloody treasure!

Aghios Emilianos

At dusk, go past the silent swimming pool
and notice that it ripples to the beat
of *rembetika* for tourists; folk-dancers
in felted cummerbunds and pleat-
ed skirts. Such hot cream tights!
See how the pompoms on their slippered feet
bob when they stamp. Now take the path
with oleander hedges, blooming whiter
in the dark. Ahead, a moonlit cataract
of thirty steps and, as you climb, the air
grows saltier. You're treading on a mush
of rose petals (there was a wedding yesterday).
Push back the studded door, feel for a chair –
and wait until the candles in their sandy tray
wake up the silver-haloed saints to glare
at dragons squirming underneath their spears
in ecstasies of anger and despair.
Incense and blackness, twinks of gold; the hush
is broken only by the throb of spray
scouring this moment, tugging you to prayer.

The Zograscope

Take this paper to the window. I know
you can't read the title at the top, because
of course it's back to front but, as I'd hoped,
you recognise the scene at once: it's a print
of Venice, the Piazza of San Marco.
The campanile's familiar, so's the three
of those five arches pointed like spears or leaves,
which top the front.
                But the view isn't from the square,
it's from a side street, round the back. Look again,
more closely: seen from behind, how hollow
those finials look! In the foreground there are groups
of men conversing (possibly eighteenth-century,
judging from their cloaks, their wigs, their white stockings).
There's a beggar sprawled on the ground, an old man leaning
on a stick. A woman leads a child.

How well do you know Venice? Don't you see,
if that's the back of San Marco on the right,
the Grand Canal (where the doges wed the sea)
should be on the left?
             It isn't; there are houses,
a pedimented church, men on a rooftop
lowering a lantern into position.
In fact, we're on a street on the other side
of the Piazza.
            The picture's left to right,
it's an engraving for a zograscope;
you can occasionally still buy one
in a junk shop (here's a photo from
an antiques magazine).
              They get mistaken
for shaving mirrors, with their mahogany
and swivelling stands. Now, if you put this picture,
this reversed scene,
            under the magnifying lens
and look at its reflection in the mirror,
you'll see so much depth and shadow
some things will loom right at you.

Weaver Bird

after Pascale Petit

I found his letters, the ones you said
he'd never sent, in a mildewed leather suitcase
beneath the cream peignoir you bought in Rome.
I'm using them to make a nest for you:
I have spread them out along the carpet
and jabbed at them with my thick beak.
The papers slither underneath my claws
and I clatter as I work. I spit and glue
just as, in restaurants when I was small,
you used to spit on damask napkins
and wipe my lips. You glued me into silence
but now I am your weaver bird, your *sa-gueng guet*,
and I will sew you into my green nest
where I've stuck the walls with fireflies
so you can read what you refused to see.
I'll hang you on a branch in the Judas tree;
your tear-shaped cage will shudder
under its silver pennies.

A Brief History of Topiary

That September, in the Garden Nursery
three hundred yew cuttings, *Taxus baccata*,
stubbled in green, were ranked
in rows of fifty, in identical brown pots.

They were like schoolgirls waiting in Assembly
cross-legged and silent in the new Sports Hall
where the morning sun cast shadows on looped ropes
and blue lines on the floor for goals and penalties.

Years later, the young yews were planted out as hedges,
so they grew together sideways, twined, supported
each other. They made a garden room for picnics,
plays, dalliance and tennis. Some had alcoves

gouged out of them, to enclose pillars or gods,
satyrs and herms. Others were cut through, so
you could look out to another garden
or to a borrowed view. A few were special:

allowed to grow above the rest, until
frames were bolted round them. When they're mature,
you don't see these underlying structures for cones,
or balls, or obelisks, or whatever.

Purists won't use frames, of course, but rely
on frequent trimming, checking from all angles.
Whichever method you chose, remember:
all stray shoots must be pinched out.

At night, the moon plays tricks on topiary,
on the giant women with their stove-pipe hats,
their capes and skirts like bells, who look as though
they'll stride off to the woods, tearing the garden down.

Every Boy his own Toymaker

So, let's make a *thaumatrope* (a spinning wonder)
from white A5-card. What pictures will you do?

On one side, the child, under a table.
Get the pose right: you're only doing an outline,

you can't get details in a silhouette. Make sure
to get the knees and shoulders sharp, the head bent.

Remember, on the back, the second sketch
is upside down. This means you're free

to map out what you know. No-one can see
both sides at once — except you, when you thread up the card

and spin it. In the book, they've drawn a bird:
its wings are spread, its head outstretched in flight.

Next, see what happens when the thaumatrope is twirled:
the bird is trapped by bars: there's a cage on the reverse

which you weren't aware of. Now, finish your designs
and whirl your spinning wonder. The images will fuse

inside your mind, you'll see what no-one else has noticed,
what won't make sense unless you put both sides together.

Look at the child underneath the table,
see how she shrinks from what is overhead.

Setting the Scene

How would a *noir* director dress your sitting-room
prior to shooting? He'd change your lighting for a start,
chuck out those ceiling saucers which cast an amber mist
speckled with dead flies; but he'd keep the nets, thick
with dust and boredom, and the shadow of a lamp-post
by the bus-stop, slicing the window like a crowbar.
If he'd had an architect like Piranesi
to etch his nightmare storyboard, there'd have been
a vaulted roof, gleams of black damp on intersecting
archways and the edges of squat engines lunging
from the dark.
        But Trauner, greatest of film-set designers,
banished the picturesque, his credo was simplicity
(albeit with receding rows of dwarves and cut-outs
made from card).
        He'd focus on the cage, the budgie with
my face, a close-up of your nails gripping my arm, leaving
a smear of machine-oil. Your eyes are flakes of slate
concealing whirring fan-blades, clacking like a clapper-board
ready for the take.

Brown Furniture

I become a cupboard, a linen
press of oak when I go
to visit you, so I don't
need to speak.
Despite your polish, the way

you spit and rub, you will never
see your face in me.
You've tried me out
in different corners, different rooms, once
even up the stairs. I've chips

and scratches from all this,
and now I won't be moved.
I dent the carpet with my clawed
feet as you shove and shove
and your eyes pop. You push

and push to get me how you want.
Then, there's the crack
of wood, a sound
of splinters. The doors fly open
like dry brown wings.

Another Lesson in Horticulture

from an ex-pupil

This tree will be your empire, giantess,
stoop and peruse its tiny canopy.
Your shouts will be its wind, your spittle, rain.
For so much sovereignty, employ
a savage diligence. Upend it
in your fist. Begin.

By clipping at its roots
you can control how far it spreads,
how far it grows.
Plant it in this shallow tray
and feed it sparingly
with gravel. Later,

you will decree
the future pattern of its branches:
rip off those leaves and buds
that intimate another, deviant,
tracery. Your policy could be
to twist and clamp the trunk,

but that's a bit overt. Instead,
push wire inside: it forms the spine
so pliant to your will.
Strip off the bark occasionally
to imitate a natural scarring.
This will embellish your design.

Westminster Tube

I thought of you this morning when
I caught the tube at Westminster: the station's
lined with stainless steel, an overcast sky
that cannot rain. The hall was huge as nightmares,

had pipes like sewers that twisted and coiled
around me, like the sinews of a giant
waiting to throttle, just as you try to squeeze
me into nothing. The barrier bared its teeth

and clamped them shut behind me so now
I'm in your head. I recognise
those transparent doors of glib politeness
which no one sees but me, how they slide

and lock; how I can't heed the red light
as I'm thrust along the black
fixed tunnels of your arguments
which always stop at the same stations.

I face the wall of grey steel where
my reflection's just a smudge, while
your rage bangs in rivets big as egg cups.
The escalator isn't working.

Batbridge

after the development of the A465 in South Wales

In the dark I learnt to navigate by echoes:

by bellowing saucepans or muttering bottles
in her wardrobe. My whispers bounced against
her anger and despair, so I pleated my wings tight.

Meanwhile, she was remodelling the house,
changing the position of doors, moving coffers
up and down the stairs where sometimes they'd stick,

tip-tilt, for days. I had to climb over,
up to the landings that she'd made,
like the stone clapper bridges that she slapped

across her arguments: *Royalty,*
nail varnish, fox hunting, the Labour Party.
Never wear a hat. That's how I learnt to swerve.

Just recently, the road out of town
has been widened and straightened. Its banks
are still raw earth, pin-pricked with seedlings.

I knew the old bridges and I'm confused
when they're removed. I need bridges
for orientation, made of rope and air.

Patient

At the door of the ward, as ordered,
I disinfect my hands. The room

holds two women; one is my mother.
The first sleeps tangled in morphine tubes;

on her tray is a pile of red noses
from her colleagues at Oxfam.

Every day she wants more —
today they're for the cleaners

yesterday it was for the doctors,
tomorrow, for the nurses. Perhaps.

The other woman sits upright,
her eyes glitter like knives

and she flinches under my kiss.
She claims she's read the book I left

(still Sellotaped up in its Waterstone's bag),
that I haven't visited before,

although she's wearing my best nightdress
and has half-finished a Duchy Chocolate Oliver

from the packet I left on her locker.
I wish I could be a radiologist,

who can stand behind a deflecting shield.
All I have is a slurp of disinfectant

as I wash my hands again, on leaving.

Lady Sackville-West expects
her Daughter Vita to luncheon

Streatham, 1932

If only, if *only*, she'd been a boy. Then
everything would have been fine, inheritance intact,
the longest drawing-room in England ready for his majority.
Instead we've got this, this striding girl with her curls
and nose, always sniffing, always poking into flowers,
her fingers squirming into the earth. Oh, she is married,
but oddly – they live separately at Sissinghurst;
little boys in one cottage, husband
next door, and she, across the lawn in her tower
with books, stained glass, a desk dotted with posies.
They meet up in the Library for meals.
She's become quite famous as a plantswoman –
husband does the layout, favouring pleached limes.
Now she's acquired a mad girlfriend novelist
who's put Vita into her latest book,
and has her change sex in the middle –
it's called *Orlando*. I hope V won't turn up dressed half-
and-half, as she did last time. Boots and breeches,
twinset and pearls. *Lady Chatterley above the waist,*
Gamekeeper below, said Osbert. And she'll sneer
(with that long dripping nose) – my garden's bare,
the beds just mud and cinders-----yes! Brenda, my dear,
I know today's your day off, but could you go
to Dickens and Jones, and buy up all the velvet flowers
in their millinery department? We could stick them
in the borders. They'd make a good show!

The Living Goddess

The Living Goddess lives in a tower
high above the Market Square. Little boys
pull us nearer, their hands soft against our sleeves
as they call out the labels they have learnt:
mädchen, lovely lady, bella donna. Their cries zigzag
up the ochre walls to a screen of fretted ebony.
Behind it, they say, stands the Living Goddess
who has never been seen. Every day
she waits there, just as she has for seven years,
and will remain until the day she bleeds.
And then she'll have to leave; she'll be about thirteen.
Nobody will want her, an ex-Goddess;
fit only for the dust of roadsides,
at best a booth by the latrines.

Already, the priests are on the look-out
for her replacement, scouring the villages,
unwrapping bundles, their long nails
fingering a baby's skin, probing her limbs.
The Living Goddess must be blemishless,
so they reject a scar, a twisted toe, a mole. They take
their tea of mountain herbs, and leave.

Line Ending

He was always plagued by line-endings. This was why he didn't lift his pencil off the paper, but kept on and on, writing more and more slowly. And his writing got smaller. When words stopped forming, he let the line go and it drew him after it, as it drew petals, the scroll of an ear, a foetus like a conch-shell. At the same time, the line annotated all these in tiny script, written backwards to bewilder him. Still he was running as the line left the page and spiralled over walls to doodle staircases, camels, a banyan tree ... then off down corridors, ambulatories, even cannons and aeroplanes. But all he had ever wanted to do was to make a lion: it walked towards the king as if to attack, then opened its mouth. And it was filled with lilies.

The Geometric Cauliflower

A different Leonardo, not da Vinci, da Pisa.

He found recurring patterns in botanic forms.

For numbers climb in spiral curve:
fir cones, shells, pineapples all serve

to illustrate this natural rhyme
in plants, though lacking thought or nerve
across the landscape and through time.

Their sequence iterates a larger tune
replicated in leaves around a stem
or ivy on a wall to catch the sun.
Rabbits in the sand, it's easy for them,
will reproduce this blueprint in the dune.

The problem lies of course in what we see:
is it an argument for a Greater Power,
illustrated, even, by the mundane cauliflower –
or is it just numbers, not a Deity?
Our mathematician lies in Italy,
his grave quite close to the Leaning Tower.
These vegetative riddles are his dower:
Leonardo, called Pisano, Fibonacci.

Chinese Painting Lesson

My ink stick
two inches long,
a thumb's width thick,
gleams like coal.

In my dish of stone,
the size of my palm,
with a teaspoon of rain
I grind it

and grind it and
grind till a black eye of ink,
thick and concave, winks;
then my fat wet brush

stains its tip,
spreads on the rice paper,
grows mountain-tops,
waterfalls, trees.

Hold-up

It was Friday, and a hundred in the shade
but my feet were cold on the marble
as I lurked in wait, and my fingers
were swollen and sticky as I snapped on
my highwayman's mask of velvet and liquorice.
You mustn't see the cracked mosaic
behind my eyes. I want you to see
my smile. I want you dazzled by the light,
I want you skidding on this glassy floor
while I climb up our memories –
grab the sudden bar your laughter swings
out to me. Then I somersault
into the sky, leaving you to admire
my slinky ankles and my trembling knees.

Jekyll Island, Georgia

White clapboard gables, big as sails, jut
above cedars.

In the dusk, pelicans distort time-frames
pterodactylly.

On the beach, egrets strut among driftwood's
statue forms.

Under the stars, palms rattle in the wind;
a hot tub steams.

Stevenson convalesced here, chose the name
for his good guy;

and we came: cycled along white dunes;
dined on the quay

by ruffling water, where the yachts
chinked their moorings

in the rising breeze which swirled the sand,
threw dust clouds in our eyes.

Back home in London, we would have our storms.
In the shadows, Hyde.

Picnic with Oysters and Earthquakes

I clamped my guilt shut like an oyster
and hurled it off the jetty.
Down it sank, to the long green weeds
and sift of sleep. Dreams weave about it,
flicking it with their orange tails.

A fisherman strides out of the sea,
he carries a trident and net.
On the breakwater, he spreads out a feast:
baguette, lemons, a bottle of Chablis.
And his knife. He watches while I eat.

Okefenokee

*This is the name the Seminole people gave to their territory
in Georgia. It means 'the land of the trembling earth.'
The Okefenokee is now a national park.*

I am in front, paddling liquid mud. Our canoe
nudges through the reeds; the air
is thick, like butter. Silence:
slop of water, quiver of insects,
Logs cruise by, and wink.

A gap in the sedge: we slide through –
acres and acres of white water lilies,
miles and miles
of sky. Silence.
The damp heat
is a second skin
while my paddle scrapes the ooze.

Back at the wharf, we tie up.
On the bank, beside the gift shop,
an alligator has clamped its jaws around a turtle.
The turtle is the size of a dustbin lid;
its paws bat the air.
Silence: then the splinter crack
of teeth through shell.

Of Cuttlefish and Candelabra

after Keith Douglas

Last week a cuttlefish
was put on the table
but only I could see that.
Someone thought
it was a spray of roses,
another a fountain
of spring snow-melt.
But I knew it for a cuttlefish,
dead and flat and hard and raspy,
waiting to stick in my throat.

Yesterday I was offered
a puddle of sago
the colour of stale tea.
It blinked at me
with a hundred weary eyes
and it trembled
its paunchy cheeks.
I was told it was a candelabra,
so I kept quiet
and my eyes shut.

Artist of the Morning Dew

When I think of you, I think of dew
and the man who swept the grass at dawn.
He brushed it into whorls,
                              a labyrinth of curves
shining as the sun rose over the stable block
gleaming gun-metal on its bell-shaped flanks,
gilding its weathervane.
                              I am too dazzled
by the leaf-blades to trace your route,
the swerve of your stories.

You don't know 'clew'? you said, surprised,
as we looked at the Minotaur in the Museum.
See also 'clue' says my OED.
                              A ball of yarn...
hence that which guides one through a maze,
an intricate investigation.

But the sun comes up too fast for me to grab the thread
and what I thought I saw dissolves, the paths that don't go
anywhere or fuse or double back.
                              You have the torso of a Minotaur.

In Summer Rain

Their mouths are always open
                              pouring water
leaving them thirsty.
                    They grip the wall
with stone claws, cannot
                        twitch their wings
to free themselves of bird-lime.

On the next wall
                the Sheila-na-gig
has a better idea:
                she opens herself
has always opened herself
                            for hundreds and hundreds
and o hundreds of years.

In this round graveyard
                        which has swallowed
hymns and dances,
                    slobber of rain
and fingers of frost
                    have gnawed her safe
from slaughter or applause.

Thirteen Gourds, a Lunar Year.

The first was that space between us
and a pause in the heat: white marble, green sea.

In the second, we stirred up memories;
like blind worms they lay, nudging, recoiling.

Third, fourth and fifth were full of laughter –
how we set them glinking in the sun!

Sixth was a jeroboam of expectation.
Seventh was the goblet of our kisses
but the eighth was full of tears.

Ninth, tenth, eleventh, were bitter cups to swallow
when we gulped down lies dissolved in fire.

The twelfth lay smashed in smithereens.
It's still there, on the cold stone.

I'm setting the lunar table for you:
I offer you thirteen gourds, chill as words.

Fireworks

On the day you die
I shall go to the bank
and take out all my savings.

On the day you die
I shall find my Yellow Pages
and look up Firework Displays.

I'll arrange with Sandling Fireworks
where and when, and confirm
payment in advance.

That night I shall lie
in the centre of your field
with my remote control.

The sky will be a crimson cape:
Fiery Demon, Raging Inferno,
a Fanned Finale of Brocade

ending with Timed Rain.
Then I shall shout
your name.

Lunar

after Les Enfants du Paradis

When the moon smiled
in a bucket of water
I pushed up my sleeves,
spun toffee-threads of story.
Red rose on a white shoe.

The river winds on rollers....
I wake, ringing a harebell
to push against the barricade
of paper-chain dancers
smiling my moon-face, churning.

New England Wedding

Hand-in-hand, through an autumn orchard
walk groom and bride

over land her forbears bought from mad King George,
ploughing up arrowheads for harvest time.

Cream lace glows up her honey skin,
the Mohegan legacy of her almond eyes.

They walk into a horseshoe that's been formed
of family and friends, who sing, recite, advise:

who offer squints into the future –
a cousin baby-old croaking a cheer,

and their best friends, new-wed six months ago,
who tightly hold hands. She's lost her hair.

Banners and trumpets, then a pumpkin feast.
Outside that curve of luck, perhaps despair.

The Faithful Couple

We walk through The Californian Tunnel Tree
cut for stagecoaches a hundred years ago.
The Fallen Monarch, the shade of cinnamon,
on whose trunk a troop of cavalry once posed
comes next, and then The Grizzly Giant,
a seedling in the age of Homer.
The grove's called Mariposa –
the Spanish word for butterfly –
but no wings shiver and the only colour,
all around, is brown. Near The Clothes Peg,
two trees with separate tufty crowns
are joined down at the base; their trunks are fused.
They will resist disease, resist decay,
but only hold the ground with shallow roots.
They could be felled by summer storm or snow,
like The Telescope, nearby. Like that, too,
they'd still bear seeds. Lightning and fire
in the burnt earth will sprout their cones.

The Hard Shoulder

Helmeted, gauntleted, you dare-devilled
the curves, your sleeves rippling, your body
squat as you leant to the bend,
your heels brushing cow parsley.

You overtook me, roaring away
to the vanishing point, insinuating
in and out of the fast lane,
the needle shivering on empty.

Evening In

After a supper of local trout
picked from the tank
and beans, sliced
over a glass of wine in the garden,
we listen to plainsong.
I knit.
We are playing at the country.

Outside the bats are still,
the air crisping,
apples hard against the moon
and the light, sharp blue, in the morning.

As we nod
by a token fire
lit only for the scent,
our minds bubble
with the day's events.
A trip to the timber mill,
a walk to Arthur's cromlech,
a pub with hop-bines, lemongrass and laverbread.

We are playing at the country:
our toy, a fast machine for cutting hedges.

How we love a bonfire!

I examine the Great Bear, and Aldebaran.
In the darkness I hear
motel music from across the valley,
a donkey snorting in the field,
screams of pain in the wood.

In Tallinn

1

An old man in a sealskin coat
with snowflakes in his hair
stoops into the Baltic wind
as he cradles a dark blue Chinese jar
and suddenly upends it:
globes of ginger in amber juice
sloop along the cobbles
and off the jetty
into the sea.

2

Snow, drifting under stone arches
was the landlord of the city
for the street was empty and the sky was dark.

And I was trespasser in this silent city,
trudging in snow-ruts, clutching at walls,
walls rough under my fingers, scabbed with old sores...

but snow had bleached the bruises
that the city absolved. And though
the street was empty and its cobbles dumb

it greeted me, intruder. On the floor
outside a door beneath an arch,
a flame burnt in a drum of oil:

open welcome for a stranger
in this silent city, where snow
is landlord and the sky's still dark.

That Bald Sexton

'Old Time the clock-setter, that bald sexton, Time.'
— Shakespeare, *King John*

1. Real Time

This is real time when, suddenly
everything goes still. Your bus has stopped
in the wrong part of town. Not
peach or lilac stucco, not piano scales
or orange blossom, but walls
of bruised concrete, where a can
knocks against the kerb
and a stained mattress leans
on a torched car. This is here
and now. And the bus driver
speaks only Polish. Everything is clear
and sharp and slow, like yesterday
on that other street:
the thud, a crash of glass,
a lorry in your back
and your head wacked
against the dashboard.

This is real time, the time in-between
when our lives are on hold,
in departure lounges, hospital
corridors or when we wait
for the phone to ring.
This is real time:
peel off from the escalator
(your family and friends ahead,
riding up to the light
with all their suitcases).
Double back to the underground,
stand again on that dark platform
and wait for a train

whose destination
is in a script you cannot read,
where strangers nod in greeting
and make a place for you.

2. Lost Time

The door says *Louka* (push)–
but you can't. Through the milky glass, see
palm trees bending, their trunks strung
with fairy lights, how they twist like dancers,
toss their tufty heads, but there's neither sound
nor scent to trigger recollection.

Peer through the pane again.
Were those branches, or were they arms
and, if so, did they wave to greet
or say goodbye? You can't go on,
you can't go back, remember.
Did those faces smile or cry?

Your sighing breath mists up the glass –
the jiggling fairy lights grow dimmer
and when they're gone, the darkness makes
a mirror – *you're* what you see: your eyes
and mouth are harder now, your cheeks less full.
Turn to the door whose sign says: *Tire* (pull).

Trip

I have been given a book of vouchers to use during my stay. I've got choices and can use the tickets for cultural activities, entertainments, restaurants and getting about. There is, however, a caveat: they must all be used up by the final date on the last page which – unfortunately – I don't have; it seems to be missing, I don't know why, but I'll find out at the end.

I was so eager to get started, I pulled off a green retail ticket and bought a pink souvenir T-shirt, with the logo. So now it shows I've been here. Because I was new, I was careful with my coupons, timid about exploring the twisting, high-walled alleys where I could see, through carved gates, courtyards with hibiscus, could smell shrimp-oil frying and hear cooks chopping leaves, or the click and snap of mah-jong tiles.

But still I couldn't read the timetables in their dusty frames; the elevator where I stayed, with its black cage and wire sides, looked unsafe. Its cables swung like monekys' tails. I tried to get to know the culture, learn the language; my feet tapped on the parquet in deserted galleries as the dust shimmered and the blinds flapped and the guards dozed beside unlabelled curves of marble; the postcards in their racks were faded and curled.

Gradually I got bolder, travelled upcountry, swam in a night sea, like milk; the fish were flakes of light, somersaulting around me; pattering on the water. Once, in a downpour, I cadged a lift on someone's crossbar. Next morning, on the lake, the merchants moored beside the houseboat, came aboard, came down to our stateroom, unrolled their carpets; suddenly light filled the room and flickered upon silks and brass and gems.

During my stay, I was much too busy to eat. I kept cutting meals, intent on exploring. I used my vouchers to buy mementoes to take back: embroideries, carved boxes, beads. I even forgot to be hungry, wrapped up in listening to the strange words, watching the strange faces. And now the book is empty. I'm hungry.

Recipe

How to do it? Wait...
until the click. Perhaps
pink phlox, how their smell smokes,
how their petals fade.

Dissolve, maybe to mist,
or low-tide mud where the river bends
or cobwebs in the dark.

And when to grow again –
push out the roots, the spark?
Like those old cars in a rotting barn,
each shedding glass and leather, cranking-shafts,
until there's just a whiff of Alvis on the floor.

Wait, wait for the rain
where it seeps through reeds,
late purple orchids and a snipe's low nest –
to the spring, a circle
which the oaks complete.

Descend to its wise chapel
and the locked door.
A recipe is also a receipt.

Acknowledgements

Many thanks to the editors of the following, in which some of these poems have appeared: *Acumen, New Welsh Review, PN Review, Poetry Wales, The Rialto.*

'Lilac' and 'A Post-it on the Microwave' were part of a pamphlet which was long-listed for the Cinnamon Press Competion in 2008: the two poems were were published in their anthology *The Ground Beneath her Feet.* 'Evening In' was part of a pamphlet collection which was a runner-up in The New County Poetry Competition for Flarestack in 1998, and was published in their anthology *Mr. Henderson to Mrs. Haut-Sinclair.*

I am extremely grateful to Tim Liardet for his wise encouragement and support.

About the Author

Ellie Evans was born in Carmarthen and was educated in Llandeilo and Cardiff. After reading English at Oxford, she worked in publishing and for the Medical Research Council, before travelling to Hong Kong, where she taught English. She has spent most of her adult life teaching in London, with extended stays in Belgium, Greece and America, but is now based in Powys, Wales. She began writing poetry six years ago, and has an M.A. in Creative Writing from Bath Spa University where she is finishing a Ph.D. Her poems have been published widely in anthologies and magazines.